The Anarchy: The History and Legacy of the Civil War in England and Normandy during the 12ᵗʰ Century

By Charles River Editors

A contemporary depiction of the Battle of Lincoln

Introduction

A 14th century depiction of King Henry I and the sinking of the *White Ship*

"We, conquered by William, have liberated the Conqueror's land." So reads the memorial to the British war dead at Bayeaux, Normandy. Commemorating those who gave their lives to free France in 1944, it also serves to remind us of an earlier conflict. For the English, the Norman conquest remains deeply embedded in the national psyche. As the last contested military invasion to have succeeded in conquering this proud island nation, the date of 1066 is the one every citizen can remember. For them, William will forever be the "Conqueror", the last invader to beat them in an open fight. For others, notably the French, he is the "Bastard", a reference not only to his lineage.

William's conquest of the island arguably made him the most important figure in shaping the course of English history, but modern caricatures of this vitally important medieval figure are largely based on ignorance. William is a fascinating and complex figure, in many ways the quintessential warrior king of this period. Inheriting the Duchy of Normandy while still an infant and forced to fight for his domain almost ceaselessly during his early years, William went on to conquer and rule England, five times larger and three times wealthier. In doing so, he demonstrated sophisticated political and diplomatic skill, military prowess and administrative acumen. Although he lived by the sword, he was a devout man who had only one wife, to whom he remained faithful.

William is one of history's most famous conquerors, but the efforts to consolidate his rule in England were complicated from the start, both due to external enemies and those jockeying for his position while he was still alive. William ultimately decided to split Normandy and England. His son Robert, still in open revolt, would nonetheless inherit Normandy, while the next in line, his second son William, would rule England. The two states that William left behind were hardly united or at peace. Soon after his death, Odo conspired with Robert to oust his brother from the English throne and re-establish a united state, but the revolt failed, and King William "Rufus" II would rule England until his suspicious death in 1100. His younger brother Henry inherited the throne, and in 1106 he imprisoned Robert after their sibling battle at Tinchebray had achieved unity once more, but any political unity would not last long.

Today, "The Anarchy" is used to describe the period in English history from the death of Henry I in 1135 to the Treaty of Winchester signed by King Stephen and his successor Henry II in 1153. Despite the name, it was an episode of civil war rather than of lawlessness and is interesting for a number of reasons, not the least of which is that it was the first time in English history that a woman claimed the throne of England in her own right. It occurred after the death of the last Norman king of England and laid the grounds for a distinctively English monarchy as opposed to a Norman colony.

This bloody era provides a fascinating glimpse into the lives, characters, and power struggles of the Norman-French nobility who had conquered England less than 100 years prior. Even as unrest and violence followed William the Conqueror's campaign, the two cultures slowly merged with each other, from modes of dress to language and political outlook. England, first under the Normans and then the Plantagenets, began to emerge as a powerful nation in its own right, rather than a divided and somewhat barbarous island off the coast of Europe, and it had an unmistakably French shading to its culture. Thus, whereas at the beginning of the struggle, England was little more than a territory of mediocre importance, by the end of the 12th century it was reunified and had the makings of a major European power.

The Anarchy: The History and Legacy of the Civil War in England and Normandy during the 12th Century examines the events that led to the fighting, and how the Anarchy shaped the future of England. Along with pictures depicting important people, places, and events, you will learn about the Anarchy like never before.

The Norman Conquest of England

The Normans, "norsemen" or "men from the north", settled in Normandy about 150 years before the birth of William. In origin, they were essentially Vikings who arrived in their longboats and decided to stay, a pattern that the nomadic conquerors also established in northern England, Scotland and even as far afield as Russia. Those who built the Duchy of Normandy would provide the catalyst for a specific culture that came to exercise a strong political and military influence over much of Europe during the early Middle Ages.

Although they were initially pagans, the Normans soon embraced Christianity and mixed with the Saxon, Celtic and Frankish inhabitants through a combination of conquest and intermarriage, to the extent that by the early 11th century, the Normans had a distinct culture that had evolved considerably from the Viking stereotype. In William's time, the Normans were renowned for their piety, architecture and martial skills. In particular, "Romanesque" Norman churches and cathedrals remain some of the most spectacular medieval structures that have survived over the centuries, and their castles were huge stone-built fortresses that helped form today's cliched view of what a castle should look like. The one at Rochester in England is a classic example, but most original Norman castles were still made of earth and timber.

Rochester Castle's keep

At the time of William's birth, his father Robert was the second son of the existing Duke of Normandy and therefore not immediately in line to inherit the duchy. Robert had taken a woman called Herlava as his wife, but the union had not been blessed by the Church, probably because of her humble background. Thus, in the eyes of the church, baby William was technically a bastard.

Statue of William's father, Robert the Magnificent

Matters might have stayed that way - and history would have turned out quite differently - if Robert had not inherited the duchy following the suspicious death of his elder brother. It is unclear whether Robert had a hand in his brother's death, but such intrigues were not uncommon in medieval Europe. 73 years later, William's own son would to suffer a similar fate in a "mysterious" hunting accident in England, thereby losing the English throne.

Regardless of how it happened, Robert became Robert I, Duke of Normandy, and he promptly married Herlava off to another nobleman and took a legitimate wife himself.[1] Herlava had two other sons with her new husband, Robert and Odo, and both would play an important part in William's life. Meanwhile, Robert I always made it clear that he expected William to inherit, regardless of his legitimacy, and his wishes were apparently broadly accepted by the Church and nobility.

---

[1] Possibly a sister of the Danish King

William was unable to influence events as a boy, and precisely when he began to directly wield power himself has proven difficult for historians to determine, but it was probably around 1042, when he was still just a young teen. That year, Henry I of France moved forces towards the southern border and demanded the destruction of the castle at Tillieres, which he claimed was a threat to French security. In no position to argue, William acceded to the request, but his man on the spot refused to surrender the castle. Matters were only resolved when William arrived on the scene in person and forced the issue, after which an uneasy treaty was signed with France. While that was obviously an inauspicious start for a ruler who would come to earn the cognomen "Conqueror", it was evidence that William had courage, political insight, and a realistic understanding of the way statecraft worked, even at that young age.

The *Anglo-Saxon Chronicle* claimed that William visited England in 1051, and it was said "William Earl came from beyond sea with mickle company of Frenchmen, and the king him received, and as many of his comrades as to him seemed good, and let him go again." He may have come to England possibly because the English King Edward had chosen him as a successor that year, but given that he was busy fighting in Anjou to the south of Normandy that same year, a trip north across the English Channel seems highly unlikely.

At the same time, Freeman noted that the situation in England and subsequent events suggest that some sort of promise was made to William around this time: "This claim is not likely to have been a mere shameless falsehood. That Edward did make some promise to William—as that Harold, at a later stage, did take some oath to William—seems fully proved by the fact that, while such Norman statements as could be denied were emphatically denied by the English writers, on these two points the most patriotic Englishmen, the strongest partisans of Harold, keep a marked silence. We may be sure therefore that some promise was made; for that promise a time must be found, and no time seems possible except this time of William's visit to Edward. The date rests on no direct authority, but it answers every requirement. Those who spoke of the promise as being made earlier, when William and Edward were boys together in Normandy, forgot that Edward was many years older than William. The only possible moment earlier than the visit was when Edward was elected king in 1042. Before that time he could hardly have thought of disposing of a kingdom which was not his, and at that time he might have looked forward to leaving sons to succeed him. Still less could the promise have been made later than the visit. From 1053 to the end of his life Edward was under English influences, which led him first to send for his nephew Edward from Hungary as his successor, and in the end to make a recommendation in favour of Harold. But in 1051-52 Edward, whether under a vow or not, may well have given up the hope of children; he was surrounded by Norman influences; and, for the only time in the last twenty-four years of their joint lives, he and William met face to face. The only difficulty is one to which no contemporary writer makes any reference. If Edward wished to dispose of his crown in favour of one of his French-speaking kinsmen, he had a nearer kinsman of whom he might more naturally have thought. His own nephew Ralph was living in England and holding an English earldom. He had the advantage over both William and his own older brother Walter of Mantes, in not being a reigning prince elsewhere. We can only say that there is evidence that Edward did think of William, that there is no evidence that he ever thought of Ralph. And, except the tie of nearer kindred, everything would suggest William rather than Ralph. The personal comparison is almost grotesque; and Edward's early associations and the strongest influences around him, were not vaguely French but specially Norman."

Either way, it's clear that William's relationship with Edward, and the issue of his succession to the English throne, would become manifestly important 15 years later.

By 1064, William had been Duke of Normandy for nearly 30 years and had been in command for at least 20 of those, but it was only by the end of that year that he considered himself fully in control of the local situation. Through the exercise of shifting alliances, bold and rapid campaigning, and even yielding when necessary, William had beaten or neutralized all of his enemies and neighbors. It was time to turn his eyes across the Channel.

In January 1066, King Edward the Confessor of England died in his palace at Winchester around the age of 60. Though he had been married for over 20 years, Edward had not produced an heir, but he apparently promised the crown of England to several people, among them Harold Godwinson and William of Normandy.

William clearly believed that Edward had promised him the throne, and this is certainly possible. Edward had spent nearly 25 years of his youth in France, mostly under the protection of William's father Robert when he was Duke of Normandy, and in 1033 Robert had gone as far as to launch a naval expedition to place Edward on the English throne. The expedition failed, and Edward would not become king until 1042, but the alliance between the two families was at that time a strong one. Notwithstanding this, the sources that claim this "promise" was made to William all come from the European continent and are dated after 1066.

Harold's claim to the throne appears to have been stronger and was universally accepted amongst the English nobility at the time. Made by Edward before witnesses on his deathbed, there is no doubt at all that his intention was to bequeath his crown to Harold, but he probably did make the earlier promise to William, and there is evidence to suggest that the fickle Edward made similar promises to others, including King Swein of Denmark.

The issue of succession was further complicated by evidence of a loyalty oath sworn to William by Harold only two years before the Battle of Hastings, in which Harold agreed to support William's claim to the English throne. Exactly why Harold traveled to Normandy in 1064 is still in dispute among historians, but it's believed William held one or two members of the Godwinson family, possibly a brother of Harold's, as hostages. Historian and biographer Jacob Abbott speculated that it may have been one of Harold's sisters, who was held as hostage through arranging a marriage between her and a Norman chieftain. While that sounds odd, it was a common practice in European medieval diplomacy as a way of ensuring rulers did not break their promises. Harold's mission may have been an endeavor to secure their release, or to confirm his support for William's candidacy to the English throne. Given that he was shipwrecked on the coast of Ponthieu, it may even be that he was not headed for Normandy at all but instead intended to visit Flanders, where one of his other brothers (Tostig) had a marriage connection.

William and his half-brothers depicted in the Bayeux Tapestry

The Bayeux Tapestry's depiction of William giving Harold arms in 1064

Regardless of how they came about, due to a complicated set of circumstances, both William and Harold had strong personal reasons for believing they had claims on the English throne in 1066. William had presumably received an earlier undertaking from Edward and had Harold's oath of support, while Harold probably resented the oath that he had been strong-armed into swearing and had subsequently heard Edward bequeath the throne to him on his death bed. As a result, the stage was set for a battle over the throne of England, and it would end up permanently changing the course of English history.

Not surprisingly, the coronation of Harold II of England on January 6, 1066 infuriated William, who summoned his noble advisors and secured their agreement for a Norman invasion of England, despite caution on the part of many of them. This was followed by a broader meeting at Caen, where William consulted his allies and built broader support for his plan.

By the summer of that year, William had assembled a large force, probably amounting to some 10,000 fighting men, with as many as 700 vessels in which to move them across the channel. His army was a decidedly mixed one, with contingents of men from Brittany, Flanders, Ponthieu and possibly even Norman allies in Italy as well. It enjoyed explicit support from the Church, with a papal banner sent from Rome, and was also therefore a triumph of diplomacy for William. More importantly, the army was a balanced one in terms of arms. The striking force would be about 2,000 heavy Norman cavalry equipped with lances, archers equipped with both conventional bows and more modern crossbows who could break up the English line, and simple infantrymen, who were lightly armored and carrying swords.

Moving a large force across the Channel was a hazardous operation in the 11th century, even without any interference from the English, but on September 27 the weather cleared and William set sail. He ensured that his own ship quickly pulled so far ahead of the fleet that in a calculated display surely meant to exude confidence, he relaxed with a heavy meal of meat and wine in the middle of the Channel while waiting for his troop ships to catch up.

It was two weeks before Harold appeared in the area, and he arrived with his forces depleted by combat and forced marching. Despite advice to the contrary, he was determined to bring William to battle as soon as possible, and he liked the battlefield as a good spot for his infantry to fight. For his part, William had been frustrated with his inability to meet his enemy in pitched battle, so with both armies in position on October 13, the night before the battle, the battle of Hastings would be a set piece one with both sides eager to win a decisive victory.

Harold largely offset his problem of numbers and fatigue by his choice of position. For an army of his type, Senlac Hill, 10 miles north of modern Hastings, was an ideal field.[2] A delineated ridge position with a steep hill to its front, difficult terrain on either flank and a wooded area behind it, the geographical features would serve to channel any attacks right into the center of Harold's line, and he would rely on his infantry shield wall to break up Norman attacks and win a battle of attrition. Meanwhile, William would use his mixture of arms by bringing up the archers to fire at the infantry lines before moving the infantry forward, with the cavalry serving as shock troops who could exploit a breakthrough. Harold hoped that fighting on the higher ground and his infantry's use of javelins would negate the effective use of cavalry.

The Battle of Hastings would last almost all day on October 14, and though it was one of the closest battles of the era, it was also one of the most decisive. Beginning at about 8:00 or 9:00 in the morning, William's archers moved forward and attempted to weaken the English line prior to an assault. Much to William's chagrin, however, the archers had little impact as the English maintained their shield wall and suffered few casualties.

---

[2] There is an emerging school which disputes this as being the actual site of the battle. See Grehan and Mace, in particular.

Norman infantry surged up the slope. "Out! Out! Out!" screamed the Anglo Saxon warriors. The clash was physical, loud, bloody. The English housecarls hacked ruthlessly at the panting Normans, adept in close quarter combat and with the clear advantage of position and protection. After less than an hour, the Bretons on William's left broke and streamed back down Senlac Hill in what was a critical moment in English history. Large groups of English troops, egged on by Harold's two brothers, romped down the hill in pursuit, but as they cut in to the fleeing Norman infantry, groups of Norman cavalry charged at the disorganized English pursuit and hit them in the flank and rear. Without formation or cohesion, the English infantry were badly mauled as they now became the pursued.

A scene from the Bayeux Tapestry depicting the fighting

The battle took a different shape as noon approached. Harold's line was ragged, with holes in it due to casualties and inadequate shield cover in parts. One of William's lieutenants suggested high trajectory archery, and this too began to take its toll as the arrows now fell beyond the protective wall and into the packed ranks behind. English casualties mounted, and having already noted the English propensity for undisciplined pursuit, William repeatedly tried to tempt them out of formation with feint attacks accompanied by the heavy cavalry.

Nevertheless, the ragged line of Englishmen continued to hold as the late afternoon turned to evening, and attack after attack was mounted up the hill, interspersed with the now deadly archery. It was at this time that the most famous event of the battle transpired. Accounts of Harold's death at Hastings differ; tradition has it that Harold was killed by an arrow in the eye, as depicted in the Bayeux tapestry, but more plausible research suggests that William and three or four accomplices picked out Harold in the denuded English line and cut their way through to him. This certainly would accord with practice at the time, as it was normal for a commander to seek his opposite number and kill him in person. Either way, once Harold was killed, his army began to disintegrate. Only the housecarls made a final stand behind a sunken lane in the woods, fighting to the last man.

The Bayeux Tapestry's depiction of Harold's death by an arrow to the eye

Looked at dispassionately, the main factor in the victory was the relative sophistication of the Norman army. It was the combination of cavalry, infantry and archery which won the day for William. It was the first time archers had been used in a battle in England, and it was clearly a triumph of the new model of warfare over the older, traditional one. Hastings ensured that the armies of Western Europe would use that model for their armies for the next 250 years. The next tactical revolution would be brought about by the English longbow, when, once again, Englishmen fought Frenchmen.

The Battle of Hastings is one of history's most famous and important battles, which is why it's widely forgotten that it did not immediately decide the issue of succession to the English throne. In fact, it took William another 10 weeks to finally secure his new crown. During this period, the northern Earls rallied more troops and attempted to put Edgar Aetheling on the throne, and there was resistance when William attempted to cross the Thames at Southwark. In response, he marched right around London, devastating crops and villages as far afield as Middlesex and Hertfordshire. This "harrying of the south" was later eclipsed by events in northern England, but nonetheless it was still very evident in the Domesday survey returns made 20 years later by William's orders.

Eventually, the English sued for peace, and the Earls recognized that it was in their interests to work with William. The nobility swore their loyalty to William, who was crowned William I of England on Christmas Day in 1066.

A Succession Crisis

William had conquered England and remains the last person to successfully invade that nation, but in 1066 he found himself ruling two states separated by 50 miles of wild sea, with plenty of enemies in each. This posed a stiff challenge for any 11th century monarch. William's solution was to establish a team of trusted subordinates in both England and Normandy, and to share his time between the two. In England, the key players were initially William's half-brother, Bishop Odo of Bayeux, who was given significant land holdings in Kent, and Roger of Montgomery, whose stronghold became Sussex. Normandy, as noted earlier, was left with his wife Matilda and his eldest son Robert Curthose.

Both domains would see a series of security threats over the first decade of William's joint rule. William returned to Normandy only five months after Hastings in March 1067, and with him he brought a group of English Earls, including Edwin of Mercier and Morcar of Northumbria, some of whom would prove troublesome later. These were essentially hostages meant to ensure the good behavior of their fellow countrymen, particulalry the remaining noblemen.

In Normandy, matters were relatively stable for the first couple of years, as William's grip on the Norman heartland was firm. When the challenges emerged, they came from familiar quarters, beginning in Maine in 1069. Le Mans revolted, and it was not long before the Anjevins began dabbling in the area, as they had over a decade earlier. The Norman garrison was ejected, and for a time Maine was effectively self-governing itself, something William could not tolerate for long. Unfortunately, William could not take immediate action there because he was engaged in more serious disturbances across the Channel.

Matters worsened in 1070 when William's brother-in-law, Baldwin VI of Flanders, died. There was a dispute over succession, and William Fitz Obern, one of William's most loyal advisors, was killed in a skirmish while attempting to intervene. Robert the Frisian became the Count of Flanders, and although he was also related to William by marriage, his regime was at best frosty towards the Normans. William had lost control of Maine and the security of a firm alliance with Flanders to the north, and to make matters worse, 20 year old King Philip of France was beginning to come of age enough to conspire against William.

With Anjou now openly assisting Maine, the time was ripe for action, but it was not until 1073 that William felt able to lead an army in person in Normandy. He had returned briefly at the end of 1071 in order to reinforce garrisons and issue defensive instructions to his commanders, but what was needed here was a punitive expedition with William at its head. In the summer of

1073, that is precisely what he initiated. His large army, for the first time, was a composite Anglo-Norman force, which was noteworthy given what had been transpiring in England during this same period. That William felt confident enough to lead in person and to assemble such a mixed force was a testament to his self-confidence. The campaign was relatively bloodless and completely successful. Launched against Maine, the rapid capitulation of Le Mans served notice both on Anjou and on the young French King. Maine was brought back under Norman rule, and William's reputation in mainland France was restored. For the time being at least, his hold on Normandy and its borders seemed to be secure.

One reason the use of an Anglo-Norman force was surprising was because William had to spend several years after Hastings struggling to control England. Despite his Christmas coronation, and the flood of loyalty oaths that came with it, William was crowned at a time when he was only truly in control of a fraction of the land. In 1066, England was a heavily divided country, ruled in practice by local noblemen, and though some of them were new blood from Normandy, many of them were figures from the Anglo-Saxon era. Naturally, there was plenty of resentment over Norman rule, and some of the revolts that William had to deal with had a nationalist flavor; but many of these conflicts were simply power struggles between warlords. In military matters, William's approach was always decisive and ruthless, but in the political settlements that followed, he emphasized reconciliation whenever and wherever he could, fully aware that England could not be held down by force of arms alone.

Ironically, the first revolt to disturb the peace in England after William's coronation was a Norman one, beginning with the Count of Boulogne assembling his followers and attacking William's garrison at Dover. Although the attempt ended up being more of a farce than a danger, it only marked the beginning. It was followed by a revolt in Northumbria, which was resolved through diplomacy, and in the west Norman troops had to lay siege to Exeter in 1068 to defuse trouble there as well. While revolts of any type naturally make leaders uneasy, these were small-scale affairs that were relatively easily suppressed or appeased. Indeed, that same year William felt safe enough to bring Matilda across the Channel and have her crowned Queen of England.

In 1069, however, the scale of uprisings entered a new dimension when two of Harold's sons, returned from exile in Ireland, attacked Exeter. Furthermore, in the north a rebelllion coalesced around the figure of Edgar Aethelring, who had been denied the crown in 1066, and his revolt was supported by a Danish invasion. There was trouble at Stafford in the midlands, as well. It was begining to look like 1066 all over again, but this time, with William in the role of Harold.

The dangers of 1068 forced William into energetic campaigning as he led forces from one threatened sector to another. The Danes, wary of facing William in pitched battle, fled across the North Sea, but they would come back in 1070, this time teaming up with rebellious English earls Edwin and Morcar and charismatic rebel leader Hereward the Wake in his eastern bastion at Ely. Peterborough was sacked by the Danes, led by King Swein, but eventually the Normans bribed them to leave England, leaving William free to deal with Hereward's force. William built a causeway across to the island on which Ely then stood and secured the surrender of the rebels.[3] Earl Edwin had by now fled north, only to be captured and killed by elements loyal to William, Morcar was imprisoned for life, and Hereward slipped away into the marshes and into English folklore.

Order had been restored, at least to an extent. William now marched his army into Yorkshire, the center of much of the opposition, and laid waste to a huge swathe of land. This was the famous "harrying of the north", traditionally seen as an excessive act of barbarism by English historians. Certainly hundreds or even thousands were killed, either directly or as a result of being made destitute, and many fled south through Evesham. While this episode is certainly unsavory in a modern context, again it was uncommon in medieval Europe, and William's conduct was exactly what would be expected of a ruler attempting to stamp out revolt in a troublesome area.

In 1071, William returned briefly to Normandy in an attempt to stabilize the situation there, but his priority remained England. King Malcolm of Scotland had been another thorn in his side, actively supporting several of the rebellions south of the border, so in the summer of 1072 William moved north. Marching confidently into the heart of Scotland, he secured Malcolm's capitulation and oath of loyalty without bloodshed, and by now his reputation as a warrior king at the head of a vaunted Norman military machine had become enough of a deterrence, at least for a few years. With peace established in England, William returned to France for his 1073 invasion of Maine.

In 1075, William faced yet another well coordinated revolt in England, this time led by two of his Norman noblemen, Ralph of Norwich and Roger of Hereford. Also implicated in the plot, though not active in it, was Earl Waltheof, until now one of William's most loyal Anglo-Saxon noblemen. Energetic as ever, William marched an army against Ralph in what is now Cambridgeshire, easily scattering his poorly disciplined insurgents. The revolt then collapsed, Ralph and Roger were imprisoned for life, and Waltheof was executed by local authorities at Winchester.

The Battle of Hastings had been followed by a tempestuous decade that left William constantly worried about security in both of his domains, but he also had to deal with civil matters. Despite the flare-ups, most of the time his subjects lived in relative peace, and William's style was to leave well alone.

As a result, Normandy continued to be governed much as it always had been, and in many ways so did England. The two currencies remained separate, as did the legal systems. England continued to be ruled through its system of local "sherrifs", while Normandy had its

---

[3] The marshes have since been drained around the modern city.

"vicomptes", who played similar but not entirely identical roles. English noblemen and churchmen, if they proved loyal, were retained; in fact, Edward the Confessor's Chancellor, Regenbald, served William in the same capacity for years, and an Englishman called Earnwig was appointed Sherrif of Nottingham in 1070. Norman noblemen and close advisors had been rewarded after Hastings with lands seized from Harold's dead courtiers, but even in those cases William allowed the families of the deceased to buy back their ancestral lands.

At the heart of William's administration was commerce. Royal holdings were effectively rented out to whoever could pay the most, allowing them to farm there as they saw fit. The "Danegeld", originally a tax levied to pay for defenses against Viking invaders, continued to be raised most years, and at a high level. Even the criminal law was used to make money; "murdrum", defined by William as the slaying of any Frenchman, resulted in a hefty fine for all of the citizens of the locality concerned. The resulting income to the Crown was not insignificant, an indication that nationalist resentment was still so high that people were willing to pay the price to spill French blood.

In addition to his lightning military campaigns, William sought to exert control by building castles, most consisting of simple log and earth structures that were bolstered with a "moat and bailey." But William also built some heavily fortified stone structures, the most famous of which is now known as the Tower of London, and it's estimated that as many as 500 castles of various types were built during William's reign.

From the mid 1070's, the circling flock of enemies which had dogged William's reign grew even bolder, and it came to include some of those closest to him. Although by medieval standards he was now an old man (in his mid-40s) and considerably overweight, his energy apparently didn't diminish, but the last decade of his life was marked less by striking military victories than by compromise and humiliation.

1076 had seen further fighting in Brittany, where Ralph of Gael was besieged by William in September, but that siege fizzled out when William, concerned at reports of a French invasion, withdrew in September. Early in 1077, Count Fulk of Anjou attacked Norman holdings in Maine, and William lacked the resources to force a decision, creating a four year military stalemate. That situation seemed to indicate William now lacked the ability to decisively enforce his will.

Perhaps sensing weakness, and clearly resenting the fact that he had no real authority of his own, William's eldest son Robert turned on him. Late in 1077, following a drunken brawl in which Robert felt he had been publicly humiliated, he rode to Rouen with a group of followers, intent on seizing William's capital. Denied access to the city, he fled to France, where the troublesome Philip was happy to give him use of a castle on the Norman border at Gerberoy. This was too much for William. At the end of 1078 he attacked his son's forces outside the castle, and in the battle itself he was wounded in a hand-to-hand fight with Robert. William pulled his troops back to Rouen, and it was there a few months later that William's wife Matilda managed to broker a reconciliation between the two.

As if to prove the sincerity of this rapprochement, it was Robert who in 1080 led his father's troops into Scotland to punish yet another incursion from King Malcolm. Malcolm again swore fealty to William and this time the treaty with the Scots would hold. Meanwhile, William's half-brother Bishop Odo, still the most powerful man in England, had to deal with an uprising in Durham.

The notion of any kind of unified Norman rule in England seemed to be slipping away, and the instability continued in France as well. In 1081, William's fortress at La Fleche was besieged, and since he was unable to intervene effectively, he had to rely on a priest to negotiate a peace treaty with the Bretons.

As if to make matters worse, Odo himself fell out of favor with William in 1083 for reasons that remain unclear. It is known that Odo was actively conspiring to take over the papacy and had kept this plot from the King, which might have posed enough of a threat in William's eyes. Either way, in an astonishing act of high political theater, William arrested his half-brother in person on the Isle of Wight. Ignoring all protestations concerning the rights of the Church (theoretically Bishop Odo was only subject to Church law), William had him imprisoned for treason.

Later that year, Matilda died, and with her went possibly the last of his old inner circle that William could truly trust. Mother to his children but also a shrewd politician in her own right, Matilda had been one of the very few who had remained loyal to William throughout. It had been a remarkable royal marriage, and her death left him completely distraught, but William had little time for mourning. Within two months of Matilda's death, his son Robert Curthose again rejected his father's rule, this time fleeing to Italy. Robert would spend the rest of his father's reign conspiring against William and attempting to raise forces to oppose him. Meanwhile, Hubert, the Vicompte of Maine, attempted to establish independence once more. William was unable to suppress the revolt and relied instead on diplomacy, ultimately persuading Hubert to sue for peace.

At the start of 1085, with Normandy surrounded by enemies on its borders and William beset by disloyalty within, he learned of a twin threat to England. There were reports that the Count of Flanders had allied with King Cnut of the Danes for a two-pronged assault on England. William's response was to levy an unprecedented Danegeld of 6 shillings per hide[4] and to recruit a large army, which he took to England. In the end neither invasion materialized, but the extremely high taxation provoked controversy at court.

---

[4] A "hide" was a piece of land deemed able to support one family; land owners were liable for the Danegeld.

It was possibly in response to this that William initiated one of the most astonishing administrative feats of medieval Europe: the Domesday book. Domesday was effectivley a nationwide land survey conducted across Norman England in 1085-86 by seven area-based commissioners. Shrewdly, William appointed senior officials with no ties to the areas they were surveying. Its purpose may have been simply taxation to ascertain exactly what taxable lands and goods existed, or it may have been for military planning and determining the resources available for future campaigns and garrisons. Other theories as to the true purpose of Domesday abound, but regardless of its purpose, William's work left history with an extremely detailed snapshot of Norman England. For example, it was from these volumes that scholars understand the extent of the damage wrought during the "harrying of the north", or the pattern of land ownership in any given parish. It is a hugely important historic resource, and astonishingly, these detalied returns were available to William as early as the summer of 1086.

It is not known precisely how William suffered the injury to his abdomen that eventually killed him, but it's likely the injury was the result of a riding accident, and that he suffered some kind of rupture which subsequently turned septic. However it happened, it quickly became apparent that the primitive medicine of the day would not save him. Taking to his bed in Rouen, he found the city too noisy, and instead had a small house built for himself just to the west. It was there that he summoned his close advisors and relatives to go about making preparations for the future of his joint realm.

William ultimately decided to split Normandy and England. His son Robert, still in open revolt, would nonetheless inherit the duchy, while the next in line, his second son William, would rule England. At the dying Duke's insistence, all of his political prisoners were to be released. Present at the death bed were the Archbishop of Rouen, his half-brother Robert, and sons William and Henry. On the morning of September 9, 1087, William the Conqueror, the Duke of Normandy and King of England, died.

William's death placed his vassals in a dilemma, for he had bequeathed the Duchy of Normandy to his rebellious son, Robert, and the Kingdom of England to his younger son, William, known to history as "William Rufus."[5] This all but ensured that those who held lands in both France and England would become torn in their loyalties, and war broke out between supporters of Robert and William II. Upon their father's death, the two agreed that one should be the other's heir, and this arrangement satisfied their anxious vassals for the time being, but it must have also been obvious to everyone involved that the arrangement would inevitably lead to political intrigue.

---

[5] Probably due to his complexion.

A medieval depiction of Robert

A medieval depiction of William Rufus

When William II died on August 2, 1100 after probably being shot by an arrow in a hunting accident or by his own men,[6] he died without leaving a direct heir. Robert might have pressed his claim to the English throne, but he had embarked on the First Crusade in 1096, leaving William Rufus, to whom he had mortgaged Normandy to pay for the First Crusade, as regent. Thus, as soon as he heard of his brother's death he hastened to Normandy, only to find that in September, his younger brother, Henry (b. 1068), had persuaded the barons of England to support him. As a result, Henry now wore the crown of England, much to Robert's fury. There was a brief peace between the two when another mutual succession agreement was concluded, but the newly coronated King Henry I was determined to take Normandy as well. After six years of undermining Robert by forming alliances with barons in Normandy, Henry invaded and defeated Robert in the Battle of Tinchebray on September 28, 1106. Robert was imprisoned, and the government of Normandy passed to Henry. Despite the victory, the title of Duke of Normandy

---

[6] <u>Frank,</u> 2000, pp. 420 – 423

did not pass to the victor, remaining with Robert until his death in captivity in 1134.

A medieval depiction of King Henry I

Another Succession Crisis

Tinchebray brought a measure of peace and security to the Anglo-Norman lands, and the Norman lords were again united under a single ruler. Henry I was an able administrator and a consummate politician, but his methods were often harsh and his dealings manipulative. His reign was by no means peaceful - he constantly campaigned against France and rebellious barons - but in general, his 35-year reign brought stability and prosperity to his English and French realms.

As previous events had indicated, however, maintaining this stability would require an heir. Shortly after becoming king, Henry married Matilda, daughter of Malcolm III of Scotland. He was 32 at the time, while she was 20. At an age when even well-fed nobles were not expected to live much past 50, Henry married later in life, but this did not indicate a reluctance to be in the company of women. In fact, Henry had numerous mistresses and 25 or more illegitimate children. Some of his sons were acknowledged and elevated to high statuses, such as Robert (born c. 1090), who was made Earl of Gloucester, but the nobles would only accept a legitimate heir. It was true that Henry's own father, William, had been known as "William the Bastard" before becoming known for all time as William the Conqueror, and William never really overcame the stigma of illegitimacy. Indeed, William had to fight hard to succeed his father and retain his rule over Normandy, and his feats could not be easily replicated by Henry I's own illegitimate son.

Initially, fears over the succession seemed to be dispelled on August 5, 1103 when Queen Matilda gave birth to a healthy boy named William. He was proudly nominated Adelin, a Gallicized version of Atheling, the title of the heir apparent used by Anglo-Saxon kings of England. As Henry's only legitimate son, he was esspecially protected and pampered. At the age of 17, he was invested with the Duchy of Normandy, and after the queen's death in 1118, he ruled England while his father was abroad.

A medieval depiction of William Adelin

William was well-educated and exposed to public life from an early age, and he was able, well-liked, and received the homage of the barons of England as *rex designates* ("king-designate"). In 1113, he was betrothed to Matilda, daughter of Count Fulk V of Anjou, an alliance that helped secure Normandy's borders. In the early 12th century, it seemed that William Adelin was destined for fortune and acclaim.

In the year 1120, King Henry I and Prince William were in Normandy along with some of Henry's illegitimate children, Matilda, Richard, and another Richard, who was Earl of Chester. One Thomas FitzStephen, captain of the newly refitted vessel *White Ship,* offered to take the members of the royal family from the Port of Barfleur back to England. The king, who had already made arrangements for himself, declined, but William and his siblings took up the offer.

It is easy to imagine the 17-year-old boy, having just been made Duke of Normandy, full of joy and *esprit* and probably eager for adventure and fun without his father watching, happily boarding the *White Ship.* The vessel, which had been recently refitted, was one of the finest available, and FitzStephen assured the prince it would reach England before his royal father, who had already set sail. The prospect of beating his father must have mischievously appealed to William, and when the ship with its royal occupants and about 300 young nobles left port on November 25, he ordered the captain to overtake the king's vessel.

William, most of his huge entourage, and the ship's crew were heavily influenced by drink, for the prince had decided to throw a party to celebrate his departure. Many have wondered why FitzStephen allowed the ship to depart, speculating that he also may have been inebriated. In fact, some of the revellers realized they were not in a condition to cross the often turbulent English Channel and disembarked before the ship set sail.

The ship eventually left port, and shortly after dark, the *White Ship* struck a submerged rock and began taking on water on the port side. Before long, the vessel capsized, during which William was taken onto a small lifeboat, but he ordered it to turn back in an attempt to rescue his half-sister, Matilda. Ultimately, everybody aboard the ship perished, including William Adelin and Matilda. One chronicler, Orderic Vitalis, claimed that the royal butcher managed to cling to the wreckage, but he allowed himself to drown when he knew the prince was dead.[7] How Orderic might have known this is unclear, but it's reasonable to assume that had anyone lived, they would have feared for their life upon having to tell King Henry the terrible news.

---

[7] Chibnall, 1978, pp. 298–299

A medieval depiction of the _White Ship_

At first, the courtiers in England would not tell Henry of the disaster, and when the news finally reached him, he collapsed with grief. The light of his life and future of England had perished, as well as his daughter, Matilda, and his other son Richard. In addition to dealing with his personal grief, Henry now had to prepare for the succession. His only other legitimate child was another Matilda, who, at the age of 12, was Empress of the Holy Roman Empire after having married Emperor Henry V in 1114. There was nothing in French law that forbade a woman from inheriting property in the absence of male heirs, despite later claims of the French kings when the kings of England claimed the throne of France, but there were pragmatic reasons for supposing that Matilda's succession would be unacceptable to the lords of Normandy and England. The Church was reluctant to crown a female in her own right, given the Scriptural doctrine holding that the man was head of his household, while the nobles were even more worried more about Matilda's husband. Theoretically, when King Henry I died, then Holy Roman Emperor Henry V would, in effect, rule the Norman domains *jure uxoris* ("by right of spouse"). Medieval nobles had no objection to owning a foreign monarch in principle (the concept of nationality did not yet exist, and political relationships were defined by feudal loyalties to persons rather than to states), but they were aware the emperor would be more concerned about affairs in Germany and Italy, not England and France. Furthermore, if Emperor Henry V died without heirs (which actually did happen in 1125), Matilda could remarry and choose a disastrous husband. For example, if she chose an English husband, the rivalries created could plunge Norman domains into civil war, such as in the days when William Rufus was regent during the First Crusade.

A medieval depiction of Henry I mourning the death of his son

A medieval depiction of Matilda

One option was to pass over Matilda and designate the nearest male relative as heir. This would be Theobald (b. 1090), son of King Henry's sister Adela and Count Stephen of Blois, Chartres, who was heir to his parents' dominions. He acquired the County of Champagne in 1125, the year of Emperor Henry V's death, and he possessed fiefs in Burgundy. Theobald was a close ally of King Henry I and could greatly enrich the Anglo-Norman realm by bringing his own lands into the fold if he was to be designated Henry I's heir.[8]

Another possibility was Theobald's younger brother, Stephen, who was born in 1092 or 1096 and was a friend and protégé of the Anglo-Norman court. King Henry I elevated him to noble rank and bestowed riches and honors upon him, but he wisely did not allow him to become so powerful he could use his status and relationship to the royal family to threaten the crown. By an ironic twist of fate, this young man, whose actions would bring dreadful misery to England,

[8] Green, 2009

should have been on the *White Ship* when it sank with Prince William, but at the last moment he disembarked and sought another ship. Henry may have been grooming him for the succession when he married Stephen to yet another Matilda, whose dowry gave him the County of Boulogne *jure uxoris*. Before then, however, Stephen's richest lands and honors were in England, meaning he would probably be acceptable to lords in England and France.

A medieval depiction of Stephen

A third candidate was favored by Louis VI of France (r. 1108 – 1137) who was, in theory, the suzerain of all players in the succession crisis. Henry I was Duke of Normandy, Theobald was Count of Blois, Chartres, and Champagne, and Stephen was a claimant to the duchy and son of a vassal of France, and these and other territories of the Kingdom of France acted as independent states. However, while the French king's authority was rarely wielded beyond the environs of Paris, he did technically retain the right to settle succession disputes, and he chose William, son of the late Duke Robert II of Normandy. This William had been captured with his father at Tinchebray in 1106 but later escaped to King Louis VI's protection.

On paper, William had a stronger claim to the thrones of England and Normandy than the other candidates. Firstly, he was the son of Duke Robert II, who had been William the Conqueror's chosen appointee in Normandy. Secondly, he was the heir of Henry I in England by reason of the mutual succession agreements Robert had made with both Henry and William Rufus. If he could be installed in Normandy with Louis VI's help, the barons in England might very well support him for the same reasons they had supported Henry: they did not want their possessions divided between two sovereigns. To further prepare William as Henry's successor, Louis endowed him with riches, married him to his half-sister, and installed him as Count of Flanders, one of France's richest provinces.

Given all the entangling alliances, designating any of these candidates as Henry I's successor would likely plunge the Anglo-Norman realm into a bloody war, so Henry I was understandably keen to try to have another son of his own. His wife Matilda, the mother of William Adelin and Empress Matilda, had died in 1118, so in 1121, Henry married Adeliza, daughter of Count Geoffrey of Louvain.

Then, in 1125, Holy Roman Emperor Henry V died without a direct heir. His reign had been a turbulent one, fighting both the papacy and princes of Germany. His wife, Matilda, found herself without a husband, but for all that, she was not powerless or vulnerable. She was a woman of considerable stature in her own right, ruling as regent in the absence of her husband and managing her estates. The dying emperor entrusted the imperial regalia to her care along with management of the succession. Still, according to custom, the German monarch was elected by the chief princes, and it was only after some difficulty that they succeeded in wresting the literal crown from Matilda's grasp. The new emperor, Lothair III, had been an enemy of her husband's, but several princes made her offers of marriage that would have secured her a place in Germany. Instead, she resolved to leave Germany and return to the land of her father. The empress had only been eight when she was betrothed to Henry, and she had spent most of her life in Germany and was probably more fluent in German than French, but she was still just 23 and doubtless envisioned a future for herself in European politics. After all, she was an empress who had ruled an empire, so if anything, it would have been more surprising if she had not set her sights on the throne of England.

Matilda spent the remainder of 1125 at the royal court in Normandy. Henry still hoped for a son by his second wife but seemed resigned to the possibility this would not happen. He summoned all of the barons of England and Normandy to Westminster (then the capital of England), where they swore to recognize Matilda and her future heirs in 1126. From experience, Henry knew that the oaths of vassals did not necessarily translate to the oaths being fulfilled, so he made arrangements for Matilda to marry Geoffrey, the eldest son of Fulk, Count of Anjou. This alliance would theoretically provide a buffer against Henry's enemies, particularly Louis VI and his protégé William, son of Robert. Matilda was reluctant to marry someone 12 years her junior, and she was an empress besides and could not be expected to marry beneath her rank.

Henry could not persuade her, though Hildebert Archbishop of Tours did succeed. He, himself, was grappling with unwelcome designs. He had been the Bishop of Le Mans in the County of Maine but was translated to the Archbishopric of Tours in 1125 by the pope, much against his will. It might be imagined that he convinced her they must both sacrifice their desires for the good of Church and State.

The marriage was difficult, even stormy. Matilda resented being married to the lowly son of a mere count, and Geoffrey disliked being reminded of her status. Their relationship was a series of long separations, rather than a union, but they remained together long enough to produce four children: Henry (b. 1133), Geoffrey (b. 1134), William (b. 1136), and Emma (b. circa 1140).

Matilda had married into a powerful family and had three sons, so the succession in her line was secure, and Henry's second marriage was still fruitless. Still, both Matilda and Geoffrey began to suspect her royal father was having second thoughts about the succession. He said nothing to contradict Matilda's claim to the throne upon his death, but he appeared to distrust Geoffrey. The couple insisted the Norman barons be made to swear allegiance as had the English at Westminster. They also wanted control of the royal castles, but the aging king, fearing a rebellion in Normandy, refused.

A rebellion broke out anyway in the south in support of Matilda and Geoffrey, led by William, Count of Ponthieu, whose father had been dispossessed by Henry. Henry personally quelled the uprising, depriving the Count of Ponthieu of his fief again, and in November, he traveled to Lyons-la-Forêt to relax and hunt. Although in good health at the age of 67, a prodigious feat in those times, he suddenly took ill and died of a "surfeit of lampreys," in his doctor's opinion, on December 1, 1135. It seems unlikely this royal fish delicacy could take the life of the longest-reigning English monarch since Ethelred the Unready, but given the state of his health, it has been speculated he might have died of food poisoning.

The Anarchy

Despite his advanced age, Henry's death caught rival claimants to the Anglo-Norman succession entirely by surprise. Matilda and Geoffrey were in Anjou when they heard of the king's death and immediately moved to seize the royal castles in southern Normandy, but many Norman barons refused to consider Matilda's claims until the king had been buried, and they resisted Matilda's further advance. Theobald, the nearest male blood relation to the late king, was at Blois, more than 300 kilometers from the English Channel. William, Count Flanders and son of the deposed Duke Robert II (who died in captivity at Cardiff the year before at the extraordinary age of 83), died of battle wounds in 1128 without heirs. Louis VI of France had backed William, but after William's death, he favored Stephen of Blois, likely opposing Matilda's claims because he did not wish to see an Anglo-German alliance. With Holy Roman Emperor Henry V dead, Louis VI likely feared a union of his powerful vassal in Anjou with the Crown of England and the coronet of Normandy.

Stephen was the only one in a position to claim England. He was at Boulogne on the French side of the English Channel, having become Count of Boulogne in 1125 following the death of his father-in-law, Eustace III. He was well-placed, not only geographically but politically, ruling vast estates in England while his younger brother, Henry, was Bishop of Winchester, one of the richest and most powerful dioceses in England. Though he had taken an oath to acknowledge Matilda, he crossed the Channel, arriving at his estate near London on December 8. The burghers of London welcomed him, and from there, Stephen advanced to Winchester, where his brother, Henry, delivered him the support of most of the bishops and the royal treasury.

The Archbishop of Canterbury, William de Corbeil, adhered to his oath to the late king concerning the succession. He was also the papal legate and could not be seen preempting the approbation of Pope Innocent II (r. 1130-1143). Stephen had to be crowned by the Archbishop of Canterbury to claim legitimacy, so Henry secured William's approval in return for a guarantee of the rights and privileges of the English Church. Henry absolved Stephen from his oath of allegiance to Matilda on the grounds that the good of the kingdom had rendered it void. At his prompting, the Earl of Norfolk, Hugh Bigod, the late king's steward, conveniently remembered that King Henry had nominated Stephen as his successor, and after that, nothing barred the coronation of the new monarch. Thus, Stephen was crowned in the presence of the peers of England with their blessings on December 26.

A medieval depiction of Stephen's coronation

Meanwhile, the barons of Normandy observed Stephen's progress with apprehension. They knew that if they supported Matilda and Geoffrey, King Louis VI, who was their king by feudal right, would probably intervene along with Stephen, but if they acknowledged Stephen, they would find themselves at war with Matilda and Geoffrey, who were already in possession of the royal castles in the duchy's south. As Stephen was gathering support in England, the Norman nobility met at Le Neuborg to consider declaring for Theobald II of Blois and Champagne. He was Stephen's elder brother and therefore had the stronger claim if only male descendants were considered, though he might split the Blois dynasty, thus weakening Stephen's position. Moreover, he was one of the most powerful noblemen in France, meaning he was capable of taking on Empress Matilda, Count Geoffrey, and Louis VI.

Theobald traveled to Normandy to negotiate with the nobles, receiving news of Stephen's coronation while taking part in the discussions. The overarching concern of the great lords was the protection of their possessions on the other side of the Channel, as it had been when William the Conqueror died, so they resolved to acknowledge Stephen. All support for Theobald evaporated, who returned to Champagne after being bought off by his brother.

Empress Matilda was at Argentan in the south of Normandy, one of Henry's castles that he had refused to hand to Geoffrey even though they were technically a part of her dowry. She does not appear to have considered conceding defeat for a moment, but Matilda had enough political experience to realize that Stephen was in a stronger position, at least for the time being. She also knew that it would not be long before his weaknesses emerged.

Sure enough, the new king was faced with an immediate war against David I of Scotland, who took advantage of the chaos to claim Cumberland and Northumbria. Stephen marched north, but rather than fight a long war rendering him vulnerable to Matilda in the south, he negotiated peace with David before journeying to Westminster to hold court on Easter of 1135. The Church and nobility expected him to reward them generously for their support, and they were not disappointed. Money was lavished on gifts and entertainment, followed by grants of land and other favors. He was careful to confirm Henry's policies that had brought prosperity and stability to the kingdom, also taking care not to disaffect the great nobles reluctant to abandon their oath to Matilda. Chief among these nobles was Robert, Earl of Gloucester (b. 1090), one of the late king's illegitimate sons. Stephen seemed secure for the time being. Louis VI preferred the House of Blois in Normandy rather than that of Anjou and acknowledged him as his vassal in the duchy. In Rome, Pope Innocent II ratified the blessing of the Church given by William de Corbeil in 1135.

However, in January 1136, a rebellion arose in south Wales. Stephen's attempts to pacify the region failed, and another revolt in southwest England forced him to abandon Wales at the end of 1137. The new revolt was led by Baldwin de Redvers, Baron of Plympton in Devon, one of the few barons refusing obedience to Stephen. After seizing Exeter, he was captured but escaped to the court of Matilda, who, in early 1136, had invaded Normandy in force with her husband.

Stephen could not leave England, but late in 1137, he was in Normandy, negotiating an alliance with Louis VI and his brother, Theobald, against Matilda and Geoffrey. He then raised an army of Norman knights and Flemish mercenaries to take Argentan, but the venture failed, and the Flemish and Normans fought each other. Stephen was forced to secure peace at the cost of 2,000 marks a year, a huge amount of money, but Stephen needed the respite. His support In England was deteriorating, the money that had lavished favors on the barons had run out, and the disastrous expedition in Normandy had emptied the treasury. Stephen promised the English bishops to restore land taken from them by William II in 1087, but most of that land was in the barons' possession, and he could not afford to offend them. He further alienated the Church by seizing the wealth of Archbishop William when he died in 1136. The Bishop of Winchester hoped to replace him in Canterbury, but Stephen feared his brother was becoming too powerful, and he nominated Theobald, Abbott of Bec in Normandy, compensating Henry by appointing him as papal legate in 1139. Theobald pledged his allegiance to Stephen and seemed willing to leave the question of Church property alone, but Henry of Blois resented the appointment, and a rift grew between the bishops of Winchester and Canterbury.

Unrest also fomented amongst the nobility. Robert, Earl of Gloucester, was one of the most powerful men in the kingdom, having ruled England when his royal father was in Normandy, and he was instrumental in William de Corbeil's nomination to Canterbury. Those disaffected or insufficiently rewarded by Stephen gravitated toward him, and in 1138, he crossed the channel to join Matilda and Geoffrey in southern Normandy. This move triggered a major revolt in Kent and a second Scottish invasion in support of Matilda, for David was the empress's uncle. The defection of her half-brother was the sign for which Matilda had been waiting. She and Geoffrey invaded Normandy, and by 1139, had subjected much of the duchy to their rule, certainly enough to consider a landing in England. Still, she hesitated, despite the Earl of Gloucester's entreaties and Stephen's considerable discomfort. Thurstan, Archbishop of York, had defeated David with a large army at the Battle of the Standard on August 22, 1138, but the King of the Scots still controlled most of the north, and the rebels halted the royal army at Bristol, despite previous losses. Dover held out, waiting for Matilda's arrival.

Matilda was still preparing her invasion forces, and besides, she was waiting for the Pope's blessing. She would have known that Innocent could hardly be expected to absolve the English barons from their oath to Stephen after releasing them from their oath to herself, but she needed to demonstrate there was a case to answer for the sake of those who were wavering. There were other reasons for hesitating. Though Stephen had been forced to concede Northumbria and Cumbria to the Scots in return for peace, he was still in a relatively strong position. He had been unable to crush the revolt in the southwest, but the revolt had not vanquished him, and the bulk of the nobility and all of the bishops stood by him. He spent 1138 and 1139 consolidating his position, creating new earldoms with considerable power and land, and appointing his most capable and loyal men to them. Waleran de Beaumont, his principal advisor and one of the first nobles to fly to his cause after the death of Henry, was made the first Earl of Worcester. De Beaumont supported his sovereign in taking action against a number of bishops suspected of wavering. The group was headed by Roger of Salisbury, Stephen's chief minister, and one of the most important figures of the realm. In tow were his nephews, the bishops of Lincoln and Ely, his son, Roger le Poer, who was Chancellor of England, and another nephew, Adelelm, who was treasurer. Roger probably had a line of communication with Matilda, but there does not seem to have been an indication he was contemplating defection. Nevertheless, Stephen could not take any chances, and he connived with Waleran de Beaumont in a conspiracy to unseat him.

In June 1139, the king held court at Oxford and set a trap for Roger. He and de Beaumont seem to have engineered a fight between Roger's retinue and one Count Alan of Brittany over lodgings in the town. It is unclear who bested whom, but the unseemly incident gave Stephen the pretext to arrest Roger's supporters and force the bishops' castles to surrender. The incident was relatively trivial, the punishment evidently excessive, and Stephen was probably sending a message to the rest of the bishops and the wavering barons. If so, he overreached himself. The king had dared to confiscate Church property, imprison Alexander, the bishop of Lincoln, and remove Archdeacon Adelelm as treasurer. The bishops were alarmed. Moreover, the Bishop of Winchester, Henry of Blois, now had a dilemma. He was the papal legate, after all, and in that capacity, he could not be seen conniving at the violation of the Church's rights.

On August 29, 1139, Bishop Henry convened a legatine court at Winchester to rule whether Stephen had erred in arresting the bishops and confiscating their property. The king did not attend personally, but he sent his chamberlain, Aubrey de Vere, to threaten the Episcopal judges. Stephen also presented the argument that there was nothing in canon law permitting bishops to possess castles, and even if it were not so, they held them by the grace of the monarch who could demand their surrender whenever he wished. Henry and the other bishops responded that the secular power had no competence judging clergy, and by long-standing law, a bishop could only be judged by an ecclesiastical court. Neither side conceded anything, but in the end, Stephen made a token act of penance while the bishops reminded him of his promises to the Church in 1135, and he retained the castles, property, and riches he had seized. The relationship between Church and state was destabilized, and the bishops never forgave the outrage committed against them.

Meanwhile, on the continent, Matilda observed developments in England and decided that the time had come to claim her throne. In August, Baldwin de Redvers crossed the English Channel with a force to the Dorset coast to secure a port for the empress. The southwest was still in revolt against Stephen, and nearby Devon was under rebel control at the time. Stephen's forces pushed Baldwin into rebel-held territory, after which the queen dowager, Adeliza—now married to William d'Aubigny, holder of Arundel, one of the newly-created earldoms—offered Matilda sanctuary in Arundel on the Sussex coast, less than 55 kilometers from Westminster.

Thanks to the generosity—and perhaps, foresight—of her late husband, Queen Adeliza was one of the most powerful and wealthy landowners in England in her own right. She enjoyed Shropshire's revenues and a large portion of London. She also possessed Chichester and numerous properties across Hertfordshire, Devon, Middlesex, Berkshire, Buckinghamshire, and

Bedfordshire. Adeliza had taken an oath to acknowledge Matilda before Henry had died, and she resented having to swear to someone she regarded as a usurper. Her husband, William, was horrified and would have nothing to do with the plot to receive Matilda. On September 30, Matilda and her half-brother, Robert, were at Arundel Castle with 140 knights and 3,000 infantry. Robert marched northwest to Bristol, expecting the land to rise in support of Matilda. His vassal, Miles of Gloucester, marched from Hereford to join him.

Stephen hastened to Arundel to lay siege to Matilda, who was surprised that he would do so given that Arundel was one of the best-fortified castles in the kingdom. At the time, it was considered virtually impregnable.[9] At that point, Henry of Blois intervened to broker a truce with Matilda, but why the king should have agreed to this is unclear.[10] The uprising against him had not been as widespread as hoped, and Matilda was trapped. On the other hand, the rebels held the southwest as far as Oxford and were within striking distance of London, and Stephen had not yet encountered Robert and Miles of Gloucester. It would probably have made no sense to tie down a large army at Arundel while needing to deal swiftly with their army. It has been suggested that Stephen allowed Matilda to leave Arundel out of a sense of chivalry,[11] yet he had shown no such courtesy toward the clergy when his authority was threatened. His brother's involvement is also a mystery, which might have had something to do with a judgment delivered by Pope Innocent II ruling in favor of Stephen. Matilda must have been stung by the argument that her mother had been a nun at the time of her marriage to King Henry, and she was, therefore illegitimate, but this spurious assertion was not accepted by the pope, who stated that he saw no reason to overturn his previous ruling in favor of Stephen. Henry of Blois was papal legate and responsible for communicating the judgment and perhaps decided Matilda should be given the opportunity to acquiesce without consequence. Then again, perhaps the Bishop of Winchester found it politically advantageous to keep Matilda at liberty.

Whatever the reason for sparing the empress, she journeyed to Gloucester under safe conduct to establish her court there, but having discharged his duty, Stephen laid siege to Wallingford, a castle on the Thames, which controlled passage along the river valley to London. He found it too well fortified and left a blockading force to march Trowbridge about 100 kilometers southwest. There, he learned that Miles of Gloucester had shattered the besieging force at Wallingford and was marching through the Thames Valley toward London. He immediately raced back to defend the capital, leaving Matilda and Robert with the secure possession of the southwest.

Stephen encountered another setback when Nigel, the Bishop of Ely in Cambridgeshire, declared for Matilda in January 1140. It must be remembered that he was nephew of Roger of Salisbury and thus no friend of the king. His uncle had died while still in the king's custody in December 1139, and Nigel blamed Stephen for his uncle's death, though there was no suggestion

---

9 Bradbury, 2009, p. 79
10 Bradbury, 2009, p. 78
11 Gillingham, 1994, p.31

he had been executed or murdered.

At the time, there was little support for Nigel's defiance, even amongst his clergy, and he was forced to take flight. Under Matilda's protection in Gloucester, he appealed to Pope Innocent to be restored to his diocese and lands, and a stalemate of sorts ensued. The east and north (save those parts conceded by necessity to the Scots) stood, by oath or compulsion, with Stephen. The general revolt hoped for by Matilda, and her allies did not occur. On the continent, Geoffrey of Anjou had not yet conquered all of Normandy. On the other hand, Matilda held the southwest and key fortresses of Wallingford, Bristol, and Gloucester. She also had Nigel of Ely, who might very well receive the support of the English Church and who was definitely supported by Innocent, but only insofar as he demanded the restoration of his position and lands. Henry of Blois stepped in once more and organized a conference between the parties at Bath, about 65 kilometers west of Wallingford. Matilda was represented by Robert of Gloucester. Stephen ended the meeting when his brother insisted that the Church would set the terms of any settlement. He felt that the bishops would use the threat of going over to Matilda to demand more power than he was prepared to give.

Thus, the fighting continued. The fact that a meeting between Stephen and Matilda occurred at all was a sign to those wavering in Stephen's camp, thinking he was in a much-weakened position. Ranulf de Gernon, Earl of Chester (1099-1153), ruled much of northern England and was forced by Stephen to surrender much of his land to King David of Scotland and his son, Prince Henry, when they invaded in support of Matilda, and he saw his opportunity to strike back at both Stephen and David. He planned to capture Prince Henry on his way back to Scotland after attending Stephen's court at Michaelmas (late September) 1140. The king got wind of the plot and sent the prince home under royal escort, whereupon Ranulf seized the royal castle of Lincoln in a fury. Stephen laid siege to the castle after initially agreeing to a truce, but Ranulf fled to his own castle at Chester on the northern border of Wales, and into Robert and Matilda's camp.

In January 1141, Stephen learned that Robert and Ranulf were marching to Lincoln with perhaps 1,500 men and decided to give battle. He had around 1,000 men, which he personally commanded, along with Alan, Earl of Richmond, and William, Earl of York. Also present were William of Ypres, Simon of Senlis, Gilbert of Hertford, and Hugh Bigold. The two forces met on February 2 outside the walls of Lincoln Castle. Robert and Ranulf, along with their vassals and Welsh infantry, charged first, almost immediately routing the enemy. The loyalist earls fled the field, and most of Stephen's barons and the king were captured. The remainder of his army took refuge in Lincoln but was pursued by Gloucester's men. The town was sacked, and the victors returned with the greatest prize they could have hoped to win: Stephen of Blois himself.

Matilda was overjoyed. She commanded Stephen be brought to her, the better to savor her victory before he was imprisoned at Bristol Castle. She then sent word to Henry of Blois, inviting the English bishops to acknowledge her and give their blessing to her coronation. She promised privately that he would have increased authority over the English Church in return for the bishops' support. He subsequently handed the Winchester treasury to Matilda, though it had been emptied by the war and Stephen's efforts to defend his crown, and began excommunicating those who refused to accept her. His authority for doing so was dubious since Pope Innocent had supported Stephen, and Archbishop Theobald, the Primate of England, adhered to his ruling with some apprehension. It was only when Matilda allowed him to see Stephen, who agreed to release him from his oath of fealty, that Theobald reluctantly submitted.

The path to Matilda's coronation was now clear. In preparation for the ceremonies at Westminster, she was proclaimed "Lady of England and Normandy." She entered London in June, underestimating the degree of resistance to her rule in that city and in the southeast of the kingdom. Few of Stephen's supporters were present for the coronation, though the city received Matilda fearfully, and justly so, as armed forces loyal to both her and Stephen had gathered beyond the city walls. Stephen's queen, also named Matilda, led his supporters.

London's unease may have been due to more than fear of soldiery and loyalty to the imprisoned king. England had never been ruled by a queen before. It was true that the wives or mothers of kings had ruled in their absence or when they were minors but never in their own right. The idea of a woman exercising power over men was considered unnatural unless she did so with her husband, but Geoffrey of Anjou was not in England, and he seems to have expressed little interest in his wife's cause, being more interested in the Duchy of Normandy. On June 24, just ahead of the scheduled coronation, London rose in rebellion, and Matilda barely escaped with her life. Queen Matilda's supporters occupied the city while the empress made for Oxford.

Matilda's cause was by no means lost. In fact, it was greatly enhanced by events in France. Louis VI of France died in 1137, and his successor, Louis VII, was at enmity with both Stephen's brother, Theobald, and Pope Innocent II. He, therefore, made an alliance with Geoffrey of Anjou that unnerved the Anglo-Norman barons—it would be only a matter of time before Geoffrey conquered all of Normandy—and they were motivated by the same anxiety that had moved them since the death of William the Conqueror, that England and Normandy would be separated and forced to give up their land. To avoid this, they were prepared to accept even a female monarch, and in England, the barons defected from Stephen in increasing numbers. Waleran de Beaumont returned to England and declared for Matilda to secure Worcestershire. Matilda's supporters, including the Bishop of Ely, were restored to their lands, and a general breakdown of the central authority ensued. Neither of the Matildas seemed capable of exerting any real authority, and the barons and bishops began minting their own coins and exercising other royal powers.

Still, it seemed the empress possessed the advantage—Stephen was still in captivity, Normandy was almost subjugated, the barons were coming to her side, and most importantly,

Henry of Blois and the bishops were behind her—yet she still endangered Henry's support by quarrelling over a cleric named William Cumin, Lord Chancellor of Scotland. King David of Scotland ruled the northern city of Durham and insisted on placing William in the vacant see of Durham against the wishes of the papal legate. Matilda wanted to offend neither David nor William d'Aumale, the Earl of York, who also supported Cumin, and he felt obliged to resist Henry. Ever jealous of his authority and seeing that the empress would not be moved, he was determined to seize control of the castle at Winchester, the royal capital in the north, and his power base. While his men laid siege to Matilda's troops, the empress set forth personally from Oxford with a small army.

Matilda's appearance at Winchester Castle was a complete surprise, not the least because women did not lead troops. Henry fled the city while his soldiers garrisoned Wolvesley Castle, situated next to Winchester Cathedral, but not before setting a large part of the city ablaze. When Queen Matilda (Stephen's wife) heard the news in London, she assembled an army of London militia, Flemish mercenary cavalry, supporters of Stephen, and feudal levies from Boulogne, and marched north. First, she cut off supply lines to the empress's army, and then, when it tried to withdraw on September 14, crushed it in an engagement known in history as the Rout of Winchester.

Empress Matilda escaped, but Robert of Gloucester was captured and refused all incentives to defect. He had been her chief supporter and the leader of his armies, and she needed him. Queen Matilda offered to exchange him for her husband, but she refused, offering 12 earls instead. In end, however, the exchange was made, and Stephen returned to London, much to the joy of its citizens.

The king's authority had, however, been severely diminished, with every baron acting as king. Matilda was defeated but not vanquished, and she was forced to abandon Oxford and establish her court at Devizes in Wiltshire. The southwest continued to stand by her—Ranulf of Chester maintained his hold on the northwest between Worcester and Carlisle, and the Scots ruled Northumbria. Hugh Bigod was still in revolt in East Anglia, and all of Normandy was under Geoffrey of Anjou's control. One of the freed king's first acts was to convene a Church council, which delivered him the bishops' allegiance, and at Christmas 1141, he and his wife were crowned again to show to the world that he was the rightful ruler of England. Beyond these symbolic events, he achieved little, his effective power extending little beyond London and its environs. Then, at Easter 1142, he took to his bed. It was widely rumored that he would not recover, and the barons began positioning themselves for the succession. His eldest son, Eustace, was only 12-years-old, and his mother would likely be regent. It was thus probable that the accession of a child-king would strengthen the empress's cause, and she took advantage of the king's illness to send Robert of Gloucester to the continent to bring back her husband's considerable army, which had conquered Normandy. This left her temporarily vulnerable, and so, it was with considerable anxiety that she learned Stephen had recovered and had taken to the field again in June.

Stephen began a campaign toward Oxford, seizing several enemy strongholds. The capture of the port town of Wareham in Dorset cut Matilda off from her allies in France, and the falls of Rampton and Bampton cut the lines of communication to Oxford. Stephen arrived at Matilda's capital on September 26, 1142. Though Matilda was present, the town was unprepared, with only the empress's armed retinue and a small force of urban militia for defense. Moreover, the castellan of Lincoln Castle had died a fortnight before and had not been replaced. Nevertheless, they offered battle at the River Witham before Stephen could begin to lay siege, but the king avoided them, navigating a series of difficult waterways and surprising the city's garrison. Stephen's men sacked Lincoln while Matilda withdrew to Saint George's Tower with a small force, but the castle was well-provisioned and fortified and could reasonably hope to stand for weeks. The rigors of winter were approaching, but Stephen was determined to starve the empress out, no matter the cost.

Meanwhile, in France, the Earl of Gloucester failed to secure Geoffrey's army. The latter had no desire to rescue his wife nor any interest in being a joint monarch of England. Gloucester returned to England with less than 400 men and immediately laid siege to Wareham, hoping Stephen would lift the siege to meet him, but he did not. Then, in December, Matilda escaped with the aid of a few knights and possibly sympathizers in the besieging army.

More amazed than furious, Stephen left Oxford with his much-weakened force and attempted—unsuccessfully—to recapture Wareham. After this, he was somewhat at a loss, for the empress was at Wallingford, a great castle that could easily hold out for a year or more, and he could not afford another long and debilitating siege. He contented himself with restoring fortifications of Oxford and attending a legatine council at Winchester in the spring of the following year, which, again, confirmed Stephen's authority, but the truth was that he had lost the impetus in the power struggle. Matilda's capture might have ended the long civil war, but she escaped, and although Stephen was in possession of Oxford, he was still, in effect, only the king of London, its environs, and the southeast, and he did not have the manpower or money to extend his dominion. For all that, Matilda was equally important. She was in secure possession of the southwest and controlled strong castles, but she did not have the strength to break out, and they reached a stalemate.

In using the term "civil war" to describe the conflict, it needs to be remembered that it was a war between the Norman and French nobility and not the English people who were Anglo-Saxons. Armies consisted of the rival monarchs' armed household, the *familia regis,* along with feudal vassals and bishops who were obliged to bring a certain number of knights. These were supported by infantry, free peasants who could afford to arm themselves—though most of the Anglo-Saxon *franklin* (freemen) and serfs remained on their lords' estates. Armies were usually quite small, rarely exceeding more than a few thousand. This was not simply due to the relatively small pool from which to recruit or the high rate of attrition due to sickness—armies were expensive to maintain for any length of time, especially so if mercenaries were hired. Indeed, armies were seldom on the move at all, their leaders preferring to besiege castles and pillage enemy territory with small bands. When armies were employed, it was to gain some important strategic advantage, and only if there was a real chance of success.

After Matilda's flight, the civil war became a bloody war of attrition, of pillage, siege, and counter-siege, with no significant gain on either side. In July 1143, one more pitched battle occurred; Stephen's last attempt to break the deadlock. He had just unsuccessfully attacked Wareham again in an attempt to cut Matilda and Robert of Gloucester from their lines of communication and supply in Normandy. He then marched some 56 kilometers northeast toward the empress's stronghold at Salisbury, halting at the Abbey of Wilton, a little over five kilometers west of the town. There, he camped and waited for the arrival of reinforcements from Winchester. In the late afternoon of July 1, sentries informed him that Robert of Gloucester was heading toward him with a sizeable army.

Gloucester's appearance was completely unexpected. Stephen believed that Matilda would not dare risk any of her precious troops in a pitched battle. The king had no time to assume battle formation before Robert's troops surrounded the walled abbey. He was under siege and would almost certainly be captured again. He resolved to sally out, and in an intense battle, struggled to break the enemy lines. Robert's cavalry drove Stephen's troops back into the abbey, dispersing them and setting fire to the abbey. The fighting dragged on till dark, and the king's steward, William Marshal, fought a rearguard action to allow his master to escape. The king disappeared into the night, but Marshal was captured. Being a chivalrous man, Stephen sought to pay his ransom, but the price was high: Matilda demanded Sherbourne Castle, a strategic fortress in Dorset.

Returning to London after his disastrous campaign, Stephen discovered that Geoffrey de Mandeville, the Earl of Essex in East Anglia, was in open revolt. Essex had been one of the earldoms created in 1139 to consolidate the king's power. When Stephen was imprisoned at Bristol, Geoffrey went over to the empress but returned to his allegiance when the king was released after the Siege of Lincoln. Stephen distrusted him, and earlier in 1143, had threatened him with execution unless he surrendered the Tower of London. He did this, but after the fiasco at Wilton Abbey, he made his displeasure openly known, marching against the royal stronghold of Cambridge with the intention of taking London, and the king could do nothing but reinforce his castles against such an assault. In early 1144, news arrived from Rouen that Geoffrey of Anjou had conquered the town, and Louis VII of France confirmed him as Duke of Normandy.

There was some good news later in 1144. Geoffrey de Mandeville died during an attack on Burwell near Cambridge in September, and Stephen came to an amicable understanding with Earl Ranulf of Chester, which drew him from Matilda's camp. Stephen's advisors distrusted the earl and counselled him to arrest the earl on charges of treason, but Stephen offered to spare him in exchange for key castles. He had done the same to Mandeville, and the outcome was the same: Ranulf returned to the field against Stephen, laying siege to Lincoln and Coventry. The king's dealings with Ranulf and Geoffrey de Mandeville soured his relationship. Even with the loyal and wavering barons, here was a monarch whose word could not be trusted.

Stephen also unwisely entered into a conflict with the Church. The bishopric of York had been vacant since 1140, and in 1144, Henry of Blois succeeded in nominating his nephew, William, as archbishop. William is believed to be the son of Emma, the illegitimate daughter of Henry and Stephen's father, Stephen II of Blois, but the archdeacons of York and the monasteries of the Cistercian Order in York objected, the latter on the grounds that their right to participate in the canonical election had been ignored. They were supported by Bernard of Clairvaux, a French Cistercian abbot and leader of the contemporary reform movement that was influential in Rome. Archbishop Theobald of Bec also opposed the election, accusing William of obtaining the see by simony and pressure from Stephen and Henry. Pope Innocent II ruled that William could take possession of the see after swearing an oath to his innocence, and despite accusations of bribery, was well-received by the people of York. He started correcting clerical abuses but was still opposed by the party of reform, led by Bernard and the Cistercians. The latter persuaded a new pope, Eugene II (r. 1145-1153), to re-examine the case. He declared that William had not been validly consecrated as a bishop on account of simoniacal practices. The ruling was a slight on King Stephen, who refused to accept William's replacement, and the rift with Rome damaged Stephen's position with the English bishops at a time when he was trying to have his son, Eustace, crowned king.[12]

Still, the war dragged on with neither side able to make significant inroads against the other. There were no notable campaigns in 1146 and 1147, with military actions being limited to sieges and pillaging. Both Stephen and Matilda's influence was negligible beyond their bases, London and Gloucester. Elsewhere, the barons were their own monarchs and often made treaties between themselves without recourse to royal authority. They built their own castles without royal permission to defend their territories. Without the royal courts, law and order collapsed, and brigands and unscrupulous barons took advantage of the chaos to steal and pillage. Trade was almost non-existent.

Neither Stephen nor Matilda sought reconciliation for the sake of the divided and bleeding kingdom. At the same time, the actual fighting between the two became sporadic and half-hearted. Robert of Gloucester died in his bed in 1147, and Matilda retired to Normandy, never to return and without renouncing her claim. In the same year, her son, Henry, now 14-years of age, crossed the channel and invaded Wiltshire. In part, the invasion failed because Henry could not

---

[12]Crowning a son while his father was still alive was a common practice in medieval Europe. Coronation secured a peaceful succession. The crowned son was considered a sort of junior king, though he usually exercised no real authority.

pay the mercenary army he had brought with him. Henry's mother seemed unaware of the venture and would not support her son, leaving him isolated and discomforted. None of the barons would give him substantial support, and in any case, many joined the Second Crusade, proclaimed by Pope Eugene III earlier in the year. Some of his most powerful allies, including Louis VII and his own father, had committed themselves. The teenager sheepishly applied to his enemy for clemency, and in a move as surprising as his granting safe conduct to Matilda in 1139, Stephen allowed him to return to Normandy. Not only did he spare the boy, but he paid off his mercenaries.

His action toward the mercenaries is understandable, as they would likely pillage the land in search of booty, yet the act of mercy for his rival challenges explanation. Commentators have pointed to the king's sense of chivalry (which apparently did not prevent war atrocities and breaches of trust with his clergy and nobles), while others suggest that Stephen realized the war would not be brought to a decisive conclusion, and he was already thinking of reconciliation with the House of Anjou.[13] If the latter was the case, Matilda, now secure in Normandy, did not share his aspirations.

Matilda's next move was to forge an alliance with Ranulf of Chester, who had acted as an independent monarch in England's northwest for several years. She confirmed the earl in his dominion and promised him the rich estate of Lancaster, as well. Matilda, Ranulf, and David of Scotland gave their support to Henry Murdac, a Cistercian cleric and friend of Bernard of Clairvaux. Eugene III had appointed him to replace Henry of Blois's nephew, William, as Archbishop of York, but Stephen refused to allow him to take possession of the city. An attack upon York—again, led by the young Henry—was planned, but Stephen's swift descent on York thwarted it. Henry returned to Normandy with his reputation and honor intact. In fact, he had developed a reputation as an energetic and capable leader, to the point where he had attracted the attention of Eleanor of Aquitaine, released from her marriage to King Louis VII on the grounds of consanguinity in 1152. Eleanor was Duchess of Aquitaine in her own right, and already, two counts had attempted to kidnap her to force her into marriage to gain her land. Henry also wanted her land, and he schemed to marry her even before the annulment of her marriage had been decided, but she was also a great beauty, and like Henry's mother, a woman of strength and ability. She may have been attracted to Henry, who was handsome, learned, and demonstrative, if fiery at times. She was 11 years older than Henry and perhaps thought she could easily influence him. Marriage with Henry would also mean the possibility of becoming Queen of England and Countess of Normandy and Anjou, and the two were wed just weeks after the annulment was finalized.

Stephen's policy now focused on the succession of his son, Eustace. For years he attempted to have him crowned, but the only person authorized to do so was Archbishop Theobald, who was, understandably, reluctant to do so. After all, both Stephen and Matilda had healthy sons, and

---

[13] Barlow, 1999, p. 180

crowning Eustace would only perpetuate the war. In 1152, Stephen attempted to force the nobles and clergy to swear allegiance to Eustace, but they refused and were imprisoned. Theobald had been papal legate since the office had been transferred from Henry of Blois in 1143, and Stephen desperately needed the support of the Church, but the archbishop fled to Flanders, where the two came to a settlement in August, and Theobald returned to England. The king was now wary of placing pressure on the Church.

Peace

In January 1153, Henry, now 21, crossed over to the north of England again, and with the support of Ranulf and Hugh Bigod, besieged the Castle of Malmesbury, about 37 kilometers south of Gloucester. He hoped to force Stephen's much smaller army to battle at the River Avon, but the king was cautious and refused to take the risk. He negotiated a temporary truce and returned to London, where he learned that Robert de Beaumont, Earl of Leicester, had declared for Matilda and was receiving Henry. Before Easter 1153, a delegation of English bishops met with him at Stockbridge, Hampshire, asking him to negotiate with Stephen, though they did not transfer their allegiance.

In July 1153, Stephen laid siege to the important stronghold of Wallingford, and for a time, it seemed it might fall, but then Henry appeared before the gates of the town with his army. For a tense while the two armies faced each other off, both of them hesitant to make the first move. The barons in both camps were weary of the war and little inclined to risk their lives and fortunes in a conflict that did not promise to end it. It had already lasted 15 years, and neither Stephen nor Matilda had the resources or means to vanquish the other. William d'Aubigney, Earl of Arundel and staunch supporter of Stephen, led the exhausted nobility, supported by Archbishop Theobald and Bishop Henry of Blois. Faced with the intransigence of his own supporters, Stephen could hardly refuse, and he agreed to a truce with Henry at Wallingford. A formal treaty was forestalled by Eustace's refusal to accept any agreement that might exclude him from the succession, and half-hearted fighting continued until November, when Eustace suddenly died; some said he was stricken by God for sacking an abbey.[14] Grieved beyond measure, the king was, nevertheless, persuaded by both his brother and the Archbishop of Canterbury to meet Henry at Winchester and negotiate a permanent peace. Stephen was to recognize Henry as his adopted son and lawful successor. Henry received certain royal castles as a guarantee, though Stephen would have free access to Henry's fortresses. Lastly, the numerous mercenaries hired on either side would be paid off and sent home. Henry and Stephen swore to uphold the treaty before the high altar in Winchester Cathedral and publicly kissed each other as a token of their reconciliation. The long conflict was finally over, but an agreement settled was no guarantee of an agreement honored. Prince William might have challenged Henry when his father died. Then again, in a time when death was swift and unpredictable, father and son might both have outlived Henry. The Treaty of Winchester seems to have contented Empress Matilda, and she never

---

[14] *Eustace,* 2004

returned to England, nor did she continue to use the title "Lady of the English." However, she did continue to govern Normandy in her son's name, and when he became King of England, she gave him important counsel.

At first, the empress opposed Henry's marriage to Eleanor, probably having recognized the woman as strong and politically able as herself, and Henry's queen did, in fact, join with his three son sons to war against him in 1173. Matilda died on September 10. 1167 at the grand old age (for that time) of 65, after having given her wealth to the Church. A woman would not wield power in her own right in England again until the short-lived Jane Grey in 1553, whose remains lie in Rouen Cathedral. She was the last of the direct line of William of Normandy, her son, Henry, having assumed the name of his father's house, that of Anjou. For this reason, the new dynasty is often called the Angevins, or Plantagenets, after a nickname given to Geoffrey of Anjou.[15]

With customary energy, King Stephen undertook great progress across England in the summer of 1154, to reassert royal authority, and the venture met with much success. Ranulf of Chester had died in 1153, but his son, Hugh, was happy to return to peace as long as he maintained the possession of his lands. King David I of Scotland also died in that year, and his successor, Malcolm IV, recognized the settlement but retained the Earldom of Northumbria from the English Crown as a nominal fief. Though Stephen was in his late fifties (or early sixties), he was still healthy and might have expected to reign for a number of years, but in the autumn of 1154, he fell suddenly ill and died in Dover on October 25.

Henry of Anjou—fearful of rumored assassination plots—was in Normandy at the time of Stephen's death. His father had died in 1151, making him Duke of Normandy and Count of Anjou, Maine, and Touraine. In addition, he was Duke of Aquitaine by virtue of his marriage with Eleanor. Already, he ruled half of France and was about to add England to his empire. Again, it is not helpful to think of Henry II as governing an English empire, as the Angevins did not think of themselves as English, but rather as a Frenchman coming into an inheritance agreed upon by treaty with another Frenchman.

Henry's landing in England was greeted with little turbulence if any. William of Blois paid homage to the new king with the other barons and bishops as he had promised, and Henry and Eleanor were crowned in Westminster Abbey on December 19. Henry's 35-year reign saw the restoration of royal authority in England, reform of the English legal system, and the hegemony over Wales and northern England. It also saw conflict with the Church, culminating in the famous murder of Archbishop Thomas Becket before the high altar of Canterbury Cathedral on December 29, 1170. Henry II also made war on France over claims in the duchies of Brittany and Toulouse to establish an English presence in Ireland. His reign was a strong, energetic, and

---

[15] Possibly after the medieval Latin name for Common Broom, *Plante Genest* (literally, "yellow flower"), though it was not until the fifteenth century that Richard, Duke of York, adopted it as a family name.

stable one, but Henry was not popular, and his death in 1189 was barely mourned. Nevertheless, he had transformed England from a backwater fought over by French magnates to a stable country and major European power.

The use of the term "Anarchy" to describe the period from 1135-1153 can be traced back to 19th century British historians, who lived in an era when Britain was a strong, stable nation-state. The British led a global empire, and moreover, the British had largely escaped the civil unrest that had recently transformed the political landscape in Europe. Looking back at that time, Matilda and Stephen's England understandably seemed lawless and ungoverned.

However, more recent historians have come to critique that analysis,[16] because the notion that there was no government at the time would have seemed incomprehensible to those who lived through it. The strict order of feudal society was not broken, as knights and peasants still had their lords, and the lords had a sovereign, whether it was Stephen or Matilda. The Church, which depended upon the Pope in Rome more than the monarch, continued to function. The baronial courts continued to administer justice even when royal power had diminished. Victorian commentators lived in a society dependent upon a strong, central authority, but in medieval England, power was shared by the sovereign, the nobility, and the Church.

Nevertheless, the civil war emptied the English royalty of much of its authority, and Henry II set about restoring and augmenting it. Though he was not, properly speaking, an English sovereign, he did much to lay the groundwork for an authentically English monarchy, particularly through legal and administrative reforms. His vast empire on the continent brought him into conflict with the kings of France, to whom he theoretically owed his French possessions, and thus was born the bitter Anglo-French rivalry culminating in the Hundred Years War. It could be said, then, that insofar as the civil war of 1135-1153 ended with the rise of Henry II, it served to start the process by which the monarchy became distinctly English rather than French. The first king of England to speak English (albeit suffused with words of French origin) was Henry IV, who reigned from 1399-1413, and it was not until 1800 that the monarch of the United Kingdom renounced his claim to French territory.

Nevertheless, to this day, in the Channel Islands, the last remnant of the Duchy of Normandy, Queen Elizabeth II is unofficially referred to as "the Duke [sic] of Normandy."[17]

Online Resources

Other books about medieval history by Charles River Editors

Other books about English history by Charles River Editors

[16] Hollister, 1994, pp. 41-45
[17] Minahan, 2009, p. 440

<u>Other books about the Anarchy on Amazon</u>

Further Reading

Barlow, Frank. (1999). *The Feudal Kingdom of England, 1042–1216. (5th edition)* Harlow: Pearson Education.

Barlow, Frank. (2000). *William Rufus* (Second ed.). New Haven: Yale University Press.

Bradbury, Jim. (2009). *Stephen and Matilda: the Civil War of 1139–53.* Stroud: The History Press.

Dyer, Christopher. (2009). *Making a Living in the Middle Ages: The People of Britain, 850 – 1520.* London: Yale University Press

King, Edmund. (2004). *Eustace, Count of Boulogne.* Oxford Online Dictionary of National Biography. https://www.oxforddnb.com/view/10.1093/ref:odnb/9780198614128.001.0001/odnb-9780198614128-e-46704.

Gillingham, John. (1994). 1066 and the Introduction of Chivalry into England. In Garnett, George; Hudsdon, John (eds.). *Law and Government in Medieval England and Normandy: Essays in Honour of Sir James Holt.* Cambridge: Cambridge University Press, p. 31.

Green, Judith. (2009), *Henry I: King of England and Duke of Normandy*, Cambridge: Cambridge University Press.

Hollister, C. Warren. (1994). The Aristocracy. In *The Anarchy of King Stephen's Reign.* Oxford: Oxford University Press.

Marjorie Chibnall (ed. and trans.). (1978). *The Ecclesiastical History of Orderic Vitalis.* Oxford: Clarendon Press, pp. 298–299.

Minahan, James B. (2009). *The Complete Guide to National Symbols and Emblems*, ABC – CLIO. https://products.abc-clio.com/ABC-CLIOCorporate/product.aspx?pc=B2180C.

Free Books by Charles River Editors

We have brand new titles available for free most days of the week. To see which of our titles are currently free, click on this link.

Discounted Books by Charles River Editors

We have titles at a discount price of just 99 cents everyday. To see which of our titles are currently 99 cents, click on this link.